I SPY

LOOK and SEE!

WELCOME TO

I SPY

LOOK and SEE!

GOOD LUCK!

I SPY with my little eye, something beginning with...

A is for AXE!

I SPY with my little eye, something beginning with...

B is for BREAD!

I SPY with my little eye, something beginning with...

C is for CAMERA!

I SPY with my little eye, something beginning with...

D and E

D is for DOOR!

E is for ELEPHANT!

I SPY with my little eye, something beginning with...

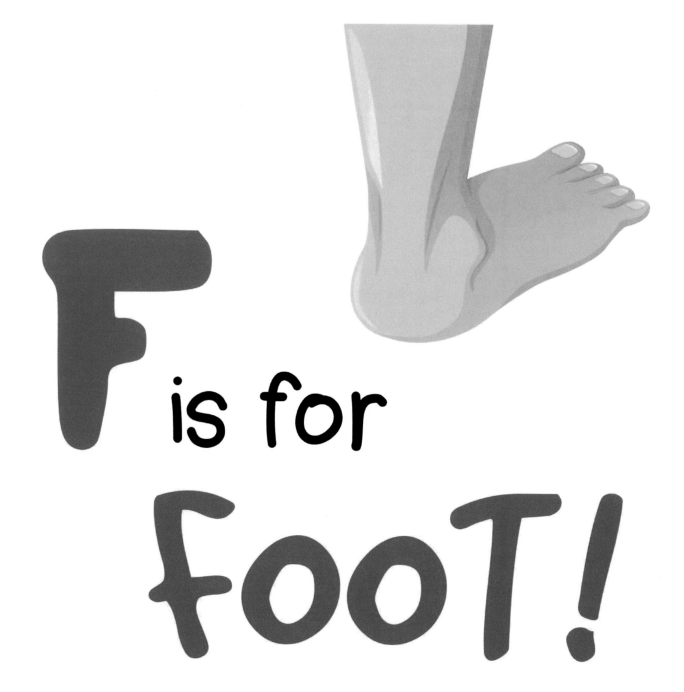

F is for FooT!

I SPY with my little eye, something beginning with...

G is for GoRILLA!

I SPY with my little eye, something beginning with...

H and i

H is for **HOSE!**

i is for **IRON!**

I SPY with my little eye, something beginning with...

J and K

K is for KEYBOARD!

J is for JAM JAR!

I SPY with my little eye, something beginning with...

L is for LION!

I SPY with my little eye, something beginning with...

M is for MOP!

I SPY with my little eye, something beginning with...

N is for NUTS!

I SPY with my little eye, something beginning with...

O is for

ONION!

I SPY with my little eye, something beginning with...

P and Q

P is for PARROT!

Q is for QUESTION MARK!

I SPY with my little eye, something beginning with...

R is for RATTLE!

S is for SEVEN!

I SPY with my little eye, something beginning with...

T is for TRUCK!

I SPY with my little eye, something beginning with...

and

V is for **VIOLIN!**

U is for **UNICYCLE!**

I SPY with my little eye, something beginning with...

W is for WEB!

I SPY with my little eye, something beginning with...

X Y and Z

X is for
XYLOPHONE!

Y is for
YACHT!

Z is for ZIP!

THE END!

Find us on Amazon!

Discover all of the titles available in the series; including these below...

I SPY ANIMALS!

I SPY EVERYTHING!

I SPY FROM A-Z!

I SPY IN THE CITY!

I SPY AT THE SEASIDE!

I SPY IN THE COUNTRYSIDE!

Made in the USA
Middletown, DE
22 February 2021